Explaining Evangelism

Steve Bowen

Sovereign World

Bible quotations marked NIV are taken from The Holy Bible, New
International Version, © Copyright 1973, 1978, 1984 International Bible
Society. Published by Hodder & Stoughton.

NASB, New American Standard Bible, © Copyright 1960, 1962, 1963 by the
Lockman Foundation.

ISBN: 1-85240-069-2

Production & Printing in England for
SOVEREIGN WORLD LIMITED
P.O. Box 17, Chichester, West Sussex PO20 6YB
by Nuprint Ltd, Station Road, Harpenden, Herts AL5 4SE.

Contents

Foreword

I know what you are thinking, 'Not another book on evangelism.' But this is a word in season. There is a new excitement as we enter the 90's that God is about to pour out His Spirit in a new measure. Elsewhere in the world revival is in progress. Here in Britain we're on the verge of a tremendous move of the Holy Spirit and the church needs to spring into action. Much has taken place through renewal in the church. Worship is coming alive, the gifts of the Spirit have come to the fore, there is a purging going on with holiness and purity becoming key words and there is a new collaboration and unity in the body of Christ. Yet, the area that still needs emphasising is the mobilisation of the church into evangelism and missions.

Steve has been a friend for many years and his enthusiasm and faithfulness in evangelism has been a constant challenge to me. In this book he has been able to bring a vast subject down to a few key principles with practical steps to take. He takes away the fear and failure mentality out of evangelism. He shows simply and clearly that we can be encouraged in evangelism if we see that our part is to be one of the links in the chain that brings a person to the Lord Jesus. We can be a success simply by sowing seeds and sowing more seeds.

Sowing seeds has a special connotation for me that goes back to 1985. As I was praying one day at Overtoun House, the YWAM training base in Dumbarton, I received a picture from the Lord. It was a picture of a jar of nice golden seeds warm, cosy and very happy there in the jar. However, their purpose in life wasn't to remain stuck in the jar. A hand unscrewed the top and pulled out three seeds. My wife Rite, my son John, and myself were the seeds. The hand took the seeds and planted them in the dark, cold, lonely earth of the west end of Paisley. Then a voice said, 'Unless a seed falls into the ground and dies it cannot bear fruit, but if it dies it bears much fruit.' I'm glad to say that those seeds are still planted and bringing forth fruit.

Like the farmer who went out to sow, as you sow with the encouragement of this book you to will 'Reap if you do not grow weary.'

Happy Sowing!!

Stephen Mayers
YWAM Director of UK and Islands.

Introduction

Over the years I have had the great joy and opportunity to lead people to Jesus. Yet, most of my joy in evangelism has come from being a seed sower. I have laid hold of the fact that there can be no reaping until sowing takes place. Someone has to sow before anyone can reap. Until I realised this truth I was frustrated at my attempts, feeling disappointment because I was not a great 'soul winner'. Then, I realised that I was very much a part of the process. It wasn't each one win one—it was the church wins one as each one does his job in proclaiming the gospel.

Evangelists, however, are those people who just seem to be able to talk about anything and people come to know Jesus. For example, in our church we had an Evangelist speak one Missions Sunday on Faith Promise Giving; during his message he simply mentioned the cross and how Jesus died for us. At the end he gave an appeal for anyone who wanted to give their lives to Jesus. To my amazement, people responded. I thought to myself, 'Evangelists could speak about bubble gum and people would get saved!'

This might be an exaggeration, but the truth remains that some are Evangelists, who have both the giftings and the callings to bring many to Jesus, and there are others who are to 'do the work of an Evangelist' (2 Timothy 4:5, NIV). I am one of the others. If you are too, then this book is for you.

In this book I will be addressing the Biblical principle of sowing and reaping in evangelism. It is my belief and experience, that this principle when applied, can free us internally to be able to sow outwardly with much freedom and joy. It is God's desire that we all become those who scatter seeds into the hearts of men.

Joyfully Sowing,
Steve Bowen

1

Get This One Fellas

Jesus, when speaking to many disciples concerning the parable of the sower, said, *'Listen! A farmer went out to sow his seed. As he was scattering the seed, some fell along the path, and the birds came and ate it up. Some fell on rocky places, where it did not have much soil. It sprang up quickly, because the soil was shallow. But when the sun came up, the plants were scorched, and they withered because they had no root. Other seeds fell among thorns, which grew up and choked the plants, so that they did not bear grain. Still other seed fell on good soil. It came up, grew and produced a crop, multiplying thirty, sixty, or even a hundred times.'* Later, Jesus said, *'He who has ears to hear, let him hear.'* Jesus then challenged and asked His disciples, *'Don't you understand this parable? How then will you understand any parable?'*

He went on to explain, to those disciples who asked, what the parable meant. In short, the sowers are men, the seed is the Word and the soils are the hearts of men at various degrees of readiness.

Later, He continues to explain what the Kingdom of God is like and just how the seed grows.

*A man scatters seed on the ground. Night and day, whether he sleeps or gets up, the seed sprouts and grows, though he does not know how. **All by itself** the soil produces corn—first the stalk, then the ears, then the full kernel in the ear. As soon as the grain is ripe, he puts the* *sickle to it, because the harvest has come.*

(Mark 4:1–29, NIV)

Jesus is driving home to his disciples the importance of this kingdom principle of sowing and reaping. If they could not get this principle into their hearts and understanding and apply it to their lives and ministry, then they would miss the mark; they would not be able to understand any other parable of the kingdom of God. We also, need to get this understanding into our minds and hearts. What is sown will grow and bear fruit. How? We don't know. It just happens. It is an unseen seed buried in the hearts and minds of men and women. Our job is to simply sow the seeds in faith.

Could you imagine a farmer after all the hours of ploughing, discing, fertilising and sowing the seeds, to go out day by day, dig up the ground to see if the seeds were beginning to grow? He wouldn't get much of a crop at harvest, that's for sure.

A good farmer sows the seed in faith, believing that all that has gone before in the preparation of the soil will bring forth a harvest. He gets the seed into the past tense and then waits patiently. He waters and allows the seeds to grow. How does it grow? *All by itself.* The seed has the power within itself to grow. The soil then produces the harvest.

This is how faith comes. Someone speaks the Word, it goes into the hearts of men and women, and in time, faith comes. Someone has to sow the Word, get it in the past tense, before someone is able to reap. *This is a spiritual reality.*

It is said that D.L. Moody, the great evangelist, never led anyone to Jesus who had not heard the gospel before. The seed had been sown before he was able to reap. This brings great encouragement to me. My job, it seems, is to be a seed sower, not to worry if the harvest is not forthcoming immediately but to sow in faith, with the view that growth will come in time.

Often, in a group setting, I'll ask the question, 'How many of you came to know Jesus the first time you heard the gospel?' Most of the time no one raises his hand. Of all the people I've had the privilege to bring to the Lord only one had not heard before. The first time she heard, faith came and she was saved. This, in the West, is not the norm. It may change in the near future, but at the present it remains true. It seems that many seeds have to be sown before a harvest can come. Consider your own life. Did you meet Jesus the first time you heard? Or, did you hear many times before making a decision? Did you need time to count the cost? To weigh up the facts? Did someone, or many people sow the seed into your life? Did another person water the seed? Who reaped the harvest of your life for Jesus? How did it happen for you? How did it happen for your friends?

This is why the call to become a sower is so important. If no one sows, and it takes one or many times for people to hear before making a decision, what will happen? Will or would the harvest be as great? If at all?

In the parable it is mentioned that the sower 'scatters' the seed. This means *many* seeds scattered. On a recent trip from America to my home in Scotland, I noticed two men in a field. They had huge baskets tied to their waists. With each step they were putting their hand into the basket, grabbing fistfuls of seed, and scattering them in front as they walked. As I was watching the men sow the seed I thought to myself, 'This is what Jesus wanted His people to do. He wants them to scatter many gospel-seed fistfuls.' This is how the harvest will come—when the seed has been sown, not before. Therefore, there needs to be *many* sowers and *many* seeds sown before a great harvest can be realised and enjoyed. The more quality seeds are sown, the greater the possibilities are for this harvest to come.

By the way, that field where the men were sowing, was

soon fully covered with barley corn. The soil produced the harvest as the men were faithful in their sowing. Jesus wanted his disciples *to get* this one. He wants us *to get* it too!

2

What You Sow Is What You Get

Many fail to realise that sowing and reaping applies to all of life. What we sow is what we will get. Some have mistakenly only applied it to financial gain. To some, 'giving to get,' is the rule. While with others it is, 'live to give'. I like the second. From my studies of the Bible it seems to me true prosperity is simply having enough to share with another in need. However, the principle of sowing and reaping does indeed go beyond financial gain.

Jesus, in Luke's gospel, says,

> *Give and it will be given to you. A good measure pressed down shaken together and running over, will be poured into your lap. For with the measure you use, it will be measured to you.* (Luke 6:38, NIV)

In context, Jesus is speaking about judging, condemning and forgiving. The implication is if we sow judgement, we will reap judgement; if we condemn, we will reap condemnation; if we sow unforgiveness, we will reap the fruit of this as well as bitterness, anger, slander and sickness. Yet, if we sow love, we will reap love; if we sow forgiveness, we will reap forgiveness and reap the fruit of forgiveness, i.e. a clear conscience, peace and joy.

As stated, this principle applies to all of life, even into the areas of friendship.

A man that hath friends must shew himself friendly.
(Proverbs 18:24, KJV)

Do you want friends? Be friendly. Do you want to be loved? Sow love. As Jesus said,

Do to others as you would have them do to you.
(Luke 6:31, NIV)

What you sow, *is* what you *will* reap.

Paul in his letters also has much to say concerning this principle. In Galatians, Paul is exhorting the saints to be aware of deception and has some straight things to say to the church. He says,

Do not be deceived: God cannot be mocked. A man reaps what he sows. The one who sows to please his sinful nature, from that nature will reap destruction; the one who sows to please the Spirit, from the Spirit will reap eternal life. Let us not become weary in doing good, for at the proper time we will reap a harvest if we do not give up. Therefore, as we have opportunity, let us do good... (Galatians 6:7–10, NIV)

We have a choice of what we sow into our lives. We can sow just to please our natural affections, or we can sow to please the Spirit of God who dwells within us. We have great choice and responsibility in this area. We can sow either good things or bad things into our lives. *If we are wanting to grow as believers we need to make sure consistent spiritual seeds are being sown into our hearts.* We need to be reading and meditating upon the Word of God, praying daily and worshipping with others.

Some, in reaction to legalism, have taught that people do not need a daily time in God's Word and in prayer, nor do they need to gather with the church. Legalistic or not, the

Bible does tell us to *'discipline ourselves for the purpose of godliness'* and to

> *Be diligent to present ourselves approved to God as workmen who do not need to be ashamed, handling accurately the word of truth. . . . Not forsaking our own assembling together, as is the habit of some, but encouraging one another; and all the more, as you see the day drawing near.*
>
> (1 Timothy 4:7; 2 Timothy 2:15; Hebrews 10:25, NASB)

This is called sowing to the Spirit. If we stop sowing into our spiritual lives, we will stop reaping and even what we think we have, will be lost. *In order to reap spiritually we have to sow to our spirits and sow consistently.* This means sowing to our spirits even when we don't *feel* like it. We are deceived if we think that we can reap spiritually if we do not sow. Legalistic? I think not. Wisdom would be the better word for this kind of sowing.

We are also deceived if we think that we can sow bad seeds into our lives and not reap a negative harvest. We cannot watch certain things on the TV (i.e. video nasties, horror films and other such movies or shows) with no effect. We cannot read or look at pornography with no effect. We cannot listen to certain music with no effect. Many would disagree with these statements. Yet, this is the very problem with deception. 'It cannot hurt my life!' is the thought. 'God cannot be mocked!' is the reality. *What we sow really is what we reap.* If we sow good things into our lives we will reap good things and if we sow bad things into our lives we will reap bad things. It is that simple. It's time that we woke up to this fact. Many would benefit in their spiritual lives if this principle was taken more seriously.

Speaking at a conference, a Pastor explaining the growth of his church said that the reason his church had grown and

15

is growing is because someone is reading the Word, some-one is praying, someone is witnessing, and someone is being faithful in the small things. In other words, someone is sowing the basics into the church life, and a harvest is being reaped as a result. To our minds, this sounds just too sim-plistic. Surely there must be more to it than this? Just to be careful to sow good things into our lives and into our churches? Just to guard our minds and spirits allowing only good seeds to be sown? To read the Word consistently, to pray daily, to sow seeds in evangelism as the opportunities arise, in word, testimony, in tract form, and to be faithful in the small things. Too simple? Would not our churches and our lives grow if these basics were sown consistently? I believe they would, for what we sow is what we reap. There are, I'm afraid, no short cuts to maintaining a healthy spir-itual life. *We are who we really are. What we have sown, is what we have reaped.*

If you have not been sowing, you can begin now. You can sow to your spirit and to your mind the Word of God. You can fan into flame the reality of Jesus through daily prayer. You can find your destiny in the Kingdom of God by being faithful in whatever small thing you are given to do, work included. If you have been sowing bad things into your life, you can by God's grace stop and turn off the supply. You need to realise that you can change. You can become what God wants you to become as you give yourself to this princi-ple of sowing and reaping.

Will it happen instantly? After all, doesn't the modern church want instant answers for instant success? Are we not products of the 'Now Generation'? Well, does seed grow in a day? Time, I'm sad to say, is needed. The soil of our hearts may need some stones removed, and some weeds taken out. Our hearts also may need to be watered by the Holy Spirit, and we may need to begin to sow some new seeds. But we will reap a harvest, if we sow, if we do not grow weary and if we do not give up.

In my office I have a small sign near my desk. It says, **'Don't Give Up. It's always too soon to give up.'** This sign sums up the attitude we need in order to see the results of sowing and reaping. The 'I don't care what happens, I won't give up', kind of attitude. This type of determination is a key to faith. Our hearts should say, 'I've decided, it's settled! My mind is made up. I won't quit! It's worth the effort. I will sow daily. I'll stand firm. Nothing will move me. I will always give myself fully to the work of the Lord, because I know that my labour in the Lord is not in vain!' (1 Corinthians 15:58).

Again, the harvest is not always instant, and time may be needed to see the desired result.

> *See how the farmer waits for the land to yield its valuable crop and how patient he is for the autumn and spring rains. You too, be patient and stand firm...*
> (James 5:7–8, NIV)

It is, 'Through faith and patience' we inherit what has been promised (Hebrews 6:12, NIV).

Keep looking for that valuable crop to come into your life and *stand firm*. The results we long to see in our lives are well worth the wait. Therefore, as we have opportunity, let us do good to ourselves, the church and the world, sowing consistently, for the harvest will come. *What you sow is what you will get!*

3

Sowing In Evangelism

It always amazes me that whenever I go to tell people about Jesus, there are usually some who have just had a close friend or someone else tell them about Him.

Recently, after going to THE GAP, a Christian outreach centre run by Inverness Youth for Christ, I met two young people who were obviously into heavy metal music. They were wearing the usual black leather jackets, T-shirts that had demons screaming off the front, tight jeans and long hair. They were drinking a couple of six-packs of beer and were in the mood for talking. I began to tell them about Jesus and what He had done for me. As the conversation went on, we drifted from Jesus, to the latest fads, music, the occult, police brutality and back to Jesus. During this time they told me that one of their friend had become a Christian recently and 'Boy he had changed!' They went on to tell me various aspects of his life and how they knew he had something they did not have. Evidently, he was clear in his challenge to them for they were pondering the issue of death before getting right with God. They had it figured out much like I had it all figured out before meeting Jesus. They had decided to wait 10 years or so to enjoy life, after all they were only 16, and then think again about giving their lives to Him. I left after a few minutes of sharing and challenging them not to wait too long. I also went away rejoicing because I recognised the hand of God in the situation. Their friend planted a seed into their hearts. I came and watered the seed. Yet, God would bring the increase as others were obedient to speak to them.

Someday some new believer may walk up to these young people and share something that touches them and they may get saved. The new believer might think, 'Boy, I'm some evangelist!' Little does he know that behind the scenes many people have been faithfully declaring God's Word to them. The Holy Spirit also has been at work convicting of sin, causing guilt to come, and drawing them to Jesus. The reality will be, seeds were sown, the seeds grew in their hearts and God brought the increase.

This is exactly what happened in my life. I was involved heavily in drinking, drugs and all that went with it. I was in the Navy and stationed in Pensacola, Florida. I was becoming more and more sick of my lifestyle, yet I could not find an escape. I was bound. Then Tim arrived—a Jesus person who was the only believer in our unit. He wore Jesus patches and spoke about Jesus whenever he had the opportunity. I used to find him interesting and talked to him often. He was continually challenging me to give my life to Jesus, but I did enjoy some of the aspects of my sin and was not willing to pay the cost. Besides, I'd just wait until the antichrist came on the scene, not take the mark of the beast on my hand or forehead, get my head chopped off and be saved in the end. He used to say, 'Why take hamburger when you can have steak?' In my thinking hamburger was easier than steak. Getting your head chopped off only took an instant, but being a believe took a life time. It was not as costly to my present life-style. After a while I stopped talking to Tim and ceased to spend time with him.

During the next three months, I became more and more miserable. Guilt was mounting because of my sin. I could not sleep, I had nightmares concerning the end times and my drug problem was growing. I had to get away. I left Pensacola and went to Kentucky to try to find some way of escape. While there I went to a party and took some drugs.

It was a bad batch and I overdosed. My nervous system went into overload. I was in bad shape.

I then had to try to drive back to Pensacola to report for my work in the Navy. As I was driving through Alabama, suddenly my life went before my eyes. I was a mess, unloved, guilty and overdosed. Then, I began to remember what Tim had told me months ago. I knew that if I died that night I would bust hell wide open. I saw the cost from a different angle. The Holy Spirit began to whisper to my heart, 'Steve this may be your last chance!' I broke, and began to weep. I pulled off to the side of the road and prayed with all of my heart, 'God help me!' At that moment, the presence of the Holy Spirit filled the car, and I knew internally that everything was going to be all right.

Two days later I met a Naval pilot who told me about how Jesus could save me and then read out these words,

For God so loved the world that He gave His one and only Son, that whoever believes in Him shall not perish but have eternal life. (John 3:16, NIV)

For the second time, I began to cry. The answer was at last clear. Later that night in his home, I surrendered to the Lordship of Jesus and was saved. That was 16 years ago.

Looking back, I can now see the times when the seed was sown and watered in my life, at vacation Bible school as a child, at Catholic boarding school as a teen and Tim. Yet God brought the increase. I'm glad He did!

All people who are saved have come to Jesus through this sowing and reaping process, unless God sovereignly saves them. People have to hear the Word before saving faith can come. Some are saved as soon as the Word is sown, and others are saved later. Yet, someone has to sow the seed.

Paul puts it this way.

How, then, can they call on the one they have not

21

believed in? And how can they believe in the one of whom they have not heard? And how can they hear without someone preaching to them? And how can they preach unless they are sent? Consequently, faith comes from hearing the message, and the message is heard through the word of Christ.

(Romans 10:14–15,17, NIV)

In Scotland as in most of Europe, many people have never heard how to be saved. This might shock some, yet it is true. Time and time again when I've shared the gospel. I have asked the question, 'Have you ever heard this before?' The answer more times than not is, 'No.' Just this week, during a teens' weekend away, I shared the good news with a 16-year-old girl. I asked her the above question and she said that she had never heard that Jesus died for her and could give her a brand new life. At 16 and had never heard!? I ask, *'Why?'* Is it because there are not many sowers sowing the seed?

Also, in doing questionnaires over the past 5 years when asked, 'Do you know what it means to be born again?' the answer is 'Reincarnation' 98% of the time, 'no' 1% of the time and 'yes' the other 1%. In Scotland, as in much of Europe, there is a great need just for sowers. If no seed is sown how can there be a harvest? Paul followed this principle of sowing and reaping in Corinth. In writing to the Corinthians he made the following observations concerning Apollos and himself.

What, after all, is Apollos? And what is Paul? Only servants, through whom you came to believe—as the Lord has assigned to each his task. I planted the seed, Apollos watered it, but God made it grow.

(1 Corinthians 3:5–6, NIV)

The first observation was Paul's confident understanding

22

of his position and role in bringing the Corinthians to faith. He, like Apollos, was a servant of the gospel through whom they came to believe. They wanted to bring the gospel to the Corinthians in a clear way so they could be saved.

Secondly, they did this as the Lord gave opportunity and assigned to each his task. Paul was the planter of the seeds. Through preaching, testifying, signs and wonders and life-style exampling he brought the Word concerning Christ to them. Apollos, in the same way of serving, watered the seed. The end result was an increase or harvest brought by God through the Holy Spirit.

Paul went on to say,

> *So neither he who plants nor he who waters is anything, but only God, who makes things grow. The man who plants and the man who waters **have one purpose**, and each will be rewarded according to his **own** labour.*
>
> (1 Corinthians 3:7–8, NIV)

He was sure to give the glory to God for the increase. He rightly understood that spiritual increase could only come by the drawing and new birth of the Holy Spirit. It was God who made things grow. This should bring encouragement to everyone who has ever sown gospel seeds. *It is up to God to cause the seeds to grow. It is His job not mine.* My job is simply to sow the seeds *in faith*, water them by prayer and leave the results to Him. The pressure is off!

Paul later says, *'We are God's fellow workers'* (1 Corinthians 3:9, NIV). We, too, are co-workers with Him. He is actively working with us and when we stop working, He remains on the job. The Holy Spirit is always at work trying to draw people to Jesus. When the seed is sown, it doesn't just lie dormant. The Holy Spirit is at work. He is convicting of sin, showing where the person is failing in righteousness. His conscience is being worked over-time and he is being made aware of the certain judgement to come. At the same time he just seems to bump into Christians at just the right moment. *God is co-working with us!* **We really do need to believe this!**

This week Edith, a lady from the church, after hearing a message on sowing, was challenged to reach out to people in her community. She prayed, 'God, what do you want me to do?' She felt like she was to go to two women in her community and share the gospel with them. One of the women was of some reputation in the community; not the best let's say. She went and knocked upon the door. No one was at home. She felt inadequate and if anyone would have been there to give her two pennies not to go back she would have taken them. But she did go back. She told the lady why she was there, shared that God had laid her specifically upon her heart and that she had come to tell her the gospel. Edith then began to share Jesus with her. The lady began to cry and asked her to tell her the reason she came again. She did and the lady began to cry more. It turns out that this woman had been going to the doctor for depression and had called out to God asking Him to show her if He cared for her and was there. You can imagine what happened within her heart when Edith showed up and began to tell her why she came.

You see, God was at work, and He is still working within her. A deep seed was sown into her life. Do you think that just because Edith walked out of the door of her house that that is the end of God's interest in this woman? No way, José! The Holy Spirit is now on the scene drawing her to Jesus and whispering hope if she would but turn to Him. He is reminding her of what Edith said.

We are co-working with Him. Can you believe it? Your sowing is important! He needs you!

Also, as Paul says, 'We have one purpose with God,' which is to bring men and women to saving faith. So that the one who sows, the one who waters, and the one who reaps might rejoice together.

After a good open air meeting where the church sang,

testified, preached the word and talked with people, a man was drawn aside for further ministry. He had had some recent problems and was looking for an answer. A friend and I were able to plant some seeds into his heart to bring him closer to Jesus. I left him my personal tract and mentioned that if he ever needed help to contact me. We parted and I felt like something good had taken place deep within him. A few months later, a pastor from the town mentioned to my pastor that this man had been saved at a healing meeting. He had hoped it didn't upset me that this man had been saved because I hadn't led him personally to Jesus. I wasn't upset, I rejoiced! I praised God that I had a small part to play in the purposes of God in his life. I understood the principle of sowing and reaping. Therefore, I could rejoice and proclaim, 'It works!'

Jesus also shared this principle in the gospel of John and brings more clarity.

> *Do you not say, 'Four months more and then the harvest?' I tell you, open your eyes and look at the fields! They are ripe for harvest. Even now the reaper draws his wages, even now he harvests the crop for eternal life, so that the **sower** and the **reaper** may be glad together. Thus the saying **'One sows and another reaps'** is true. I sent you to **reap** what you have not worked for. Others have done the hard work, and **you have reaped the benefits of their labour.*** (John 4:35–38, NIV)

Jesus in this illustration, I believe, was not only pointing to the white fields ready for harvesting but was pointing to the men coming towards him from the town. These men were ripe for harvest, which later proved to be true. The disciples, I'm sure, rejoiced when these men believed in Jesus. They had entered into the labours of Jesus and the woman who had done the initial sowing, the hard work. They all rejoiced together as this spiritual harvest came.

Again, our job is to sow seeds *in faith*, looking to reap. But if reaping does not come immediately we can find joy in doing our part in planting and watering the seed.

4

Bring 'em Down The Scale

Several years ago at a large outreach in Edinburgh, Paul Filler of Youth with A Mission, shared with us a simple diagram which helped explain the process of sowing and reaping. I have greatly benefited from this illustration as have many others. It is easy to understand. If applied, it can help all of us in our efforts in bringing people to Jesus. I'll pass it on to you.

| -100 | | -50 | | -10 | -5 | 0 | +5 |

This graph shows how the principle of sowing and reaping operates. The minus (−) side is where people are in relation to salvation. Plus one (+1) would be salvation into the kingdom of God. People we contact day by day are somewhere along this plane. Our job, with the Holy Spirit co-working with us, is to bring people closer to saving faith in Jesus.

If, for instance, we meet an atheist who claims not to believe in God, we might be foolish (unless led by the Holy Spirit) to try to immediately ask him if he wants to be saved. He probably doesn't even know He's lost. It would be wiser to sow the seeds where he is in his concepts and thinking, than to draw him down the scale as far as we are enabled. If for instance we had a good talk and he admitted he thought that there could be a God beyond his limited understanding, then, we should rejoice! He is no longer at −100 but at −90. The next Christian he comes into contact with may be enabled to bring him to a −50 and so on.

Soon after I heard this teaching, I met a young doctor named Paul from Canada. He was sitting on the steps of a museum on the Mound in Edinburgh. I began to share Jesus with him and found out that he was a Catholic but had never understood the gospel, yet was searching. After our talk he invited me to tea, and over the meal we continued our conversation about the things of the Lord. He was very interested. A few days later I returned to his house with a book by Larry Tomczak entitled *Clap Your Hands*. It was Larry's story of how he, being a good Catholic, came to know Jesus. This book helped Paul greatly and watered the initial seed moving him closer to Jesus. After several more conversations, over a period of a few days, I knew that I had to return home. So, I made sure that Paul was put into contact with a good Spirit-filled church in Edinburgh. Several weeks passed, and then I received a letter from Paul telling me of how he began to go to this church and had finally made a choice to follow the Lord Jesus. One of the members of the church had continued to talk with Paul and brought him into saving faith.

This story shows the way this graph can work. If I had not understood this principle, I could have become discouraged at my efforts to evangelise Paul. However, I was able to water the seeds already planted into Paul's heart by the Catholic church. He was probably at −50 on the scale. He had a concept of God and an awareness of sin. Through our continued conversations and reading Larry's book, he may have been brought to −20. By the working of the Holy Spirit, the preaching of the Word and through the love and care of the members of this good church, his heart may have been moved to −5. At just the right time a specific person was able to pray with him and God brought the increase as

Paul was born again, now a +1 in the Kingdom of God. He is now married to a great Christian girl and has returned to Canada to live. Paul came to Jesus progressively as people were faithful to water the seed that was sown into his heart. As you can see, **the pressure is off! Our job is to *sow* and water the seeds *in faith!*** It is the Holy Spirit's job to bring the increase!

At this point it is also important to remember the apostle Paul's exhortation, *'Each one should be careful how he builds'* (1 Corinthians 3:10, NIV).

We need not only to witness with words but with our lives as well. It is possible to send people running back up the negative scale. If we are ungracious, uncaring, unloving and insensitive in our witness we may do more harm than good. We need to understand evangelism is about bringing people with real needs and with sin, to a God who loves them and is interested in their lives. The Holy Spirit woos, and the kindness of God does lead many to repentance. We do need wisdom about how to speak to every person. People are very different and no two are the same. The Four Spiritual Laws may work for some but might not work for others. It is having sensitivity and wisdom that causes us to be a good witness. Proverbs says, *'. . . He who wins souls is wise'* (Proverbs 11:30, NIV).

During an outreach in Falkirk, Scotland we had with us a Canadian team of teenagers who after being taught this scale and the principle of sowing and reaping, began to go and to sow. We had a great time. The summer weather was hot, a miracle in itself, and were able to do most of the outreach in shorts. We had many lengthy talks in the town centre and on one of the housing estates. We also sang, did drama and preached. It was challenging to believer and nonbeliever alike because of the teenagers who were taking part. They were from the ages of 14–17, and fiery. You get extremely challenged when a girl of 14 gets up to speak in front of hundreds without fear, and with anointing, I might add. We were on a seed sowing expedition for two weeks. During this time, not many came to know Jesus, but all of us were full of joy. We knew without condemnation and without a doubt that we had done our job. We had sown many seeds. Many of these seeds went into the lives of people who had never heard the gospel before.

This was the principle of sowing and reaping in action. Some sowed and others would reap, yet we can rejoice together as the Holy Spirit does His work.

One day during the outreach I stopped a young man and asked him if he'd like to answer some questions. He said, 'Yes.' So we began to talk. It was interesting. His grandmother had just finished sharing the gospel with him a few days earlier, and here was another person talking to him about Jesus. During the conversation I sensed the presence of the Holy Spirit and asked him if he thought there was someone else with us as we were talking. He acknowledged this fact and stated that this was the reason he was still talking to me. We had a lengthy talk, and at the end I asked if there was anything I could pray with him about. He said he had a toothache and allowed me to pray. I asked if I could put my hand on his shoulder. He said, 'OK.' As I began to pray he just looked me in the eyes. (I think unbelievers want to make sure everything is alright and nothing funny happens, so they pray with their eyes open. I don't think God is threatened. I wasn't.) The Holy Spirit touched him. He then knew that God was real and interested in him. I didn't get to lead him to Jesus but could nevertheless rejoice in the wisdom and love of God!

The call is clear. We need sowers to sow the seed before there can be a reaping. If we are looking to see a harvest of people come into our churches, someone, somewhere, has to go and sow the seeds. Who will do it? Any answers?

5

Hindrances To The Call To Go And Sow

Every believer senses the inner prompting to share their faith. We all know that we should go and tell others about Jesus. It is a desire and drive that is prompted by the Holy Spirit who dwells within us. It is His job to bring glory to Jesus and to empower us for the purpose of witnessing to the uttermost parts of the earth. He wants to flow out of us and into the world. Our job is to cooperate with Him.

When I first met Jesus I was full of zeal and wanted everyone to know that He had saved me. I couldn't wait to be baptised, to attend church and to witness to others. As a matter of fact, I witnessed to anything that moved and was very vocal. Jesus had delivered me from drugs and my old life, I was into something brand new and I wanted everyone to know it. Many of my friends and family thought I'd cracked up. Time, however, was on my side. I really did change and the change was evident to all. Jesus had saved me! It wasn't a passing fad. I've stuck it out and through time have been able to tell most of my family and friends the good news.

It has been my experience that many new converts are just like I was, unashamed and bold. Probably more people hear the good news the first few years of a believers life in Jesus than at any other time. Why? The reasons are many, but the words and phrases that come to mind are: First Love, Unashamed Joy, A Sense of Purpose and the Great Commission. New believers have many of these new concepts moving around inside of them which propel them into evangelism. They also have a hunger for God's Word and pray a great deal for friends and family. They want others to have what they have! Therefore, they are not hindered but free to share the good news. 'Oh! To be born again, again!' might be the prayer of some. Yet, many of us who once were 'On Fire' have now been hindered from going. What are the hindrances that keep us from going and sowing? Here are some which may help us to return to those 'early days'.

You've lost that loving feeling

Our lives are like a large fountain which spills over into all of life. If we are having a fresh, loving relationship with Jesus and are continually being filled with His Spirit and His love, we cannot help but share that which fills our lives and hearts. This overflow extends to our families, our churches and out to the world we live in.

Jesus said,

> *Those who are forgiven much love much.* (Luke 7:47)

This is one of the reasons why new believers are so powerful. They have a fresh revelation within them of what Jesus has done for them. They are assured of His kindness expressed by His forgiveness. They know that God loves them because Jesus died for them, they have experienced a new birth and all things are brand new. Therefore they are simply sharing this new life out of the overflow.

Many are hindered in their efforts to reach the lost simply because they have left or lost their first love. Jesus is no longer their number one affection; something has come in and crowded Him out of their lives. There is no fresh revelation of His love and forgiveness. Therefore, there is a lack of abundance within their hearts, and there is no overflow.

We need to return to Jesus with all of our hearts, to ask the Holy Spirit to fill us and to fan into flame a new hunger and love for Him. As we return, new life will once again fill our lives and an overflow will more likely take place. We will not be able to keep from speaking about the One who has loved us with an everlasting love. We will overflow. Our words will have life and we will be sharing out of the abundance.

You're a believer? Shame on you!

One of the biggest traps that the enemy and the world can bring to a believer is a false sense of shame, which brings fear, thus hindering our sowing. Have you ever noticed how you feel, in certain situations, when it becomes known to your family, friends or workmates that you are a 'Christian'? Is it a sense of shame?

There have been many times when I've been in situations where this conflict comes. I might be at a party full of unbelievers. Everyone is drinking and getting drunk and I'm not. Some might try to project shame upon me for not joining in. Or I might be at an open air meeting proclaiming the good news. Some might be opposed to what I am doing. The sense is almost always the same, 'Shame on you.' If I receive it, this false sense of shame will hinder my effectiveness as a sower.

Timothy had this same problem. He had to work through his own insecurities and fears in order to evangelise. Paul, knowing him well, exhorted him:

> *Keep your head in all situations, endure hardship, do the work of an evangelist...* (2 Timothy 4:5, NIV)

Earlier in this letter Paul encouraged Timothy to *'fan into flame the gift of God.... For God did not give us a spirit of timidity, but a spirit of power, love and of self-discipline.'* He was saying to Timothy to be bold; to not allow fear or timidity to rob him and others of God's giftings and blessings. He went on to say, *'So do not be ashamed to testify about our Lord...'* (2 Timothy 1:7–8, NIV). It appears that Timothy may have been struggling with this false sense of shame that hindered him from boldly testifying about the Lord Jesus. Paul exhorted him not to give in to fear and shame but to recognise the spirit of power, love and self-discipline he had within.

Many are like Timothy. Shame and fear may have bound them. They are not free to sow. However, God wants us to rise up and shake away all that hinders. He wants us unashamed and bold. *Shame is a trap of the enemy.* We need to remember Jesus's warning,

> *If anyone is **ashamed** of me and my words in this adulterous and sinful generation, the Son of Man will be ashamed of him when he comes in his Fathers glory with the holy angels.* (Mark 8:38, NIV)

I have come to the conclusion that we as believers do not have anything to be ashamed of. *How can we be ashamed of the One we love?* Jesus is the one who loved us and gave up His life that we might live. Besides, we are the ones that are attempting to live sinless lives. We don't cheat, get drunk, sleep around or lie, or shouldn't that's for sure! We have peace with God, Jesus has cleansed us from our sins and we are attempting to live in right relationship with others. What do we have to be ashamed of? Absolutely nothing! Those who try to make us feel ashamed are the ones who should feel ashamed, not us. Therefore, don't receive the shame when it is put upon you. Stand up, look them straight in the eye, smile, and internally acknowledge you have nothing to be ashamed of. Say with Paul,

I am not ashamed of the gospel, because it is the power of God for the salvation of everyone who believes.
(Romans 1:16, NIV)

Why, you are the righteousness of God in Christ Jesus and the righteous are as bold as lions. 'You aren't right with Jesus! Shame on you!' should be our thought. 'Jesus, now help me to love and reach this person,' should be our prayer.

Apathy and indifference

This is the greatest disease ever released into the church. It is the 'I cannot be bothered' attitude of the heart and mind. This disease probably robs more churches of their life and vitality than any other. I believe that this sense of apathy and indifference is a real spiritual force that needs to be broken in our lives and from our people. It lulls us to sleep. What at times is needed is a good hard slap in the spiritual face!

There is an old after shave commercial that I like. A man just gets out of bed in the morning. He staggers into the bathroom and begins to look into the mirror. He slowly shaves while yawning. He finishes shaving. Suddenly, a hand appears from nowhere and smacks the man in the face with the after shave. He was drowsy but is now wide awake. He exclaims, 'Thanks! I needed that!'

We also need short, sharp shocks to cause us to wake up. We need the prophetic word to come to us and to our churches. We need to see the reality of the situation. We need to wake up! Jesus is returning soon! Men and women are dying and going to Hell! We are living in urgent times! If we don't wake up and begin to sow the good news, who will? We are God's plan to reach man! We are all that He has got! The church is it! We may say, 'Yes, that's right. The church should begin to do it.' I ask, 'Who is the church?' Got a mirror? Have a good look!

There is a great illustration from a well known pastor. A young man walked into his office visibly upset. He began to vent his frustration at what the 'church' was not doing. It seems he had met a man who had no place to stay, so he provided a room for him. The man had no money, so he gave him some money. The man had no transport to look for a job, so he drove him around town. Now he was upset because the 'church' wasn't doing it's job. The wise pastor leaned back and smiled and said, 'I think that the church is doing a pretty good job.' After a pause, the penny dropped into the heart of the young man. *He was the church. So are you! Understand?*

Don't allow the spirit of apathy and indifference to take control of your life. Rise up! Shake yourself! Move ahead! Be the church! Begin to sow! If it's going to be, it really is up to thee!

We don't have it together yet

Many people and churches are waiting to reach out because they don't have 'it' together yet. The reality is, if they know Jesus, they have it much more together than the people they are trying *not* to reach. Besides, when will 'it' ever be totally together? One year? Two? Ten? How many opportunities have been lost for the sake of getting 'it' together?

When I was young in Jesus and had become a bit disillusioned with my efforts to reach out and with the church I attended (I then didn't understand who or what the Church was), I made a statement to a missionary from Honduras who was visiting. I said, 'Ed, what do we have to offer the lost anyway? I mean look at us. We're a mess.' I'll never forget his kind rebuke. He simply said, 'Jesus'. This one statement really sums it up. We have salvation to offer a lost and dying world in Jesus name. He is the One who puts things together. He makes the puzzle fit and He is the one

36

who is building His Church. Without Him people are lost, with Him they can be saved. A person who has been born again for just one day has more life than those who have not. They are getting 'it' together because Jesus is in their lives. They now have a future and a hope, the lost do not.

If we are waiting for the church to get 'it' together we will be waiting a long, long time. There will *always* be a need for improvement in our lives and in our churches until Jesus returns. As the saying goes, 'If you find the perfect church don't go to it, because once you are there it will not be perfect any more.'

We need to understand that God's heart beats two ways—toward the lost and toward His Church. He wants His Church to be built and He wants the lost to be reached. He wants both. This is where many make the mistake. They emphasise building the church at the expense of reaching the lost or emphasise reaching the lost at the expense of building the church. Both should go hand in hand. As the Church is being built, the lost should be being reached, and as the lost are being reached, the Church should be being built. (By built, I don't necessarily mean a brick building but the people being built together as living stones.)

We also need to understand the reasons for our existence as a church. We exist for the world. The world doesn't exist for us. As we are getting 'it' together we need to realise who we are getting 'it' together for. We exist to be a people and a place where others can be added and discipled. We exist to be a place for them. The Church is where they learn to love and worship God and to serve each other. It is where they realise that there is a purpose for their lives and that they can join in God's eternal purpose in reaching the nations. The Church exists to be a blessing to God and to the world. Israel missed it. Will we?

Why not sow now as you are getting 'it' together? It seems right to me and I'm sure Jesus won't mind either.

Not clear of the call

Some might not go because they 'have not heard the call.' It might be better stated, 'Some are not going because they might not be listening.'

As someone once said, 'The great commission is not the great suggestion.' It was not an afterthought, 'By the way fellas, be sure to go into all the world and make disciples.'

Jesus throughout His life and ministry demonstrated the heart of God toward the lost of the world. He came into the world to heal, deliver and save sinners. He also trained His disciples by being with them and sending them out on short term mission trips. They learned to do what He did and to feel as He felt.

Before going to the Father, Jesus commissioned or commanded his disciples. It was not a suggestion.

> *As the Father has sent me, I am sending you.... All authority in heaven and in earth has been given to me. Therefore go and make disciples of all nations.... Go into all the world and preach the good news to all creation.... Repentance and forgiveness of sins will be preached in His name to all nations.*
>
> (John 20:21; Matthew 28:19; Mark 16:15; Luke 24:47, NIV)

We need a specific word from God *not to* share our faith instead of one *to* share our faith. If you are walking down a street, in a shopping centre or speaking with your neighbour and the thought comes to your mind or heart to share the good news, don't rebuke it! It is most probably the Holy Spirit. If you as a church decide to do some sort of evangelism, you don't have to wonder if God wants you to share with others or if it is His will. Of course it is! He has given us a command! Some super-spiritual people want to make sure they are 'led' to do evangelism. Therefore, if they don't 'feel led' they won't go. I often wonder if they have 'led poisoning'. Responding to the great commission is not a matter of 'feeling led', but one of obedience. He has already spoken. Are we listening? 'Go,' He has said. We just need to obey.

Some are not responding to the call because they want to do power evangelism. They may never have said boo to a bug, but want to 'power evangelise'. So again, they wait until they have 'it together' in this area before going. I'm all for 'power evangelism', and we really do need the power of the Holy Spirit to see the desired results. However, we need to begin to 'Go' in the natural, to break into the supernatural. The greater always comes out of the lesser. It is going *now* and being faithful to what God has already said that will bring us into the greater. Remember, 'Go' is a command, not a suggestion.

What hinders you?

What is it that hinders you in your evangelistic efforts? Is it one of the hindrances that I've mentioned? Or is it something else? Whatever it is that hinders you, be determined to press through to become a seed sower. Jesus needs you! The world needs you! Therefore rise up, and be determined to begin to sow life changing seeds into the lives of the men and women around you, *NOW! You really can do it!*

6

Seeds Corporately

In our efforts to witness there are many different seeds we can sow. Some are more important than others, yet all are legitimate seeds. Some are seeds that whole churches can sow in their community as a corporate body of believers.

In our church we have endeavoured to sow seeds into the community to let people know that we exist and that Jesus is the answer. I call this *Visibility Evangelism*.

First of all, if no one knows where you meet how can they, if in need, get in contact with you? Therefore, we have endeavoured to use the local newspapers for advertising Sunday meetings and special events. We have had several people come and join us as a result of these ads. One lady came to an evening we had exposing the cults. She had been thinking about joining the Jehovah Witnesses. After seeing the ad in the paper for this special meeting she decided to come. During the teaching time that night, she realised that the Jehovah Witnesses were not for her and that Jesus was the answer she had been looking for. During a time of ministry she decided to give her life totally to Jesus. Since then she has become one of the greatest soul winners of the church.

Secondly, we have monthly open-air meetings where we as a church go into the High Street. We praise, worship, dance, do drama, have a muppet show, testify, preach, have one on one talks and hand out hundreds of contact tracts which explain a little bit about who we are, what we believe, and where we meet. Inside each tract there is a simple gospel message explaining the way of salvation. In front of our gathering we have a board that tells who we are and where we meet. The open-airs enable us to sow personal seeds into the lives of many people and also raise our corporate visibility. Does it work? The answer is, 'Yes!' There are some people who have been saved at the open-airs, and there have been people who have been added to our church by coming to our meetings as a response to our contact tracts. In many conversations people say, 'Oh you're the church that meets on the High Street.' We say, 'Yep, that's us!' Recently, one of the ladies from the church was approached in a restaurant and asked, 'Well, what are you doing today?' She replied to this total stranger, 'I'm working.' The stranger said, 'It isn't what you were doing last week, that's for sure!' It turns out that this person had seen the open-air and had walked by, stopped and listened to the singing and the testimonies. She was impressed by the joy she saw and heard, had noticed this lady, and was now asking her some questions concerning the church. Seeds sown!

Thirdly, we have been active in sponsoring the National Bible Society on a Saturday during the town's yearly Civic Week. We have a colourful booth that looks like the Dunfermline Abbey-of sorts, and we hand out free gospels and hundreds of contact tracts. We also raise money for the Bible Society by charging people for throwing wet sponges at us. You'd have to see it to believe it! It's estimated that over 20,000 people are in attendance on the day. Many of these walk by our booth. As a result, we are becoming known more and more in the community, the gospel has got out and the Bible Society has been blessed.

Lastly, we have endeavoured to promote church unity over the years, joining with other churches for Celebrations, meeting with other full time leaders and doing joint outreaches. At Easter we join with many other churches from the town in putting out an Easter leaflet through every door in the city. The leaflet has a gospel message, testimonies of local people and the names of the participating churches.

Consistency

The key word and principle for this type of evangelism to succeed is CONSISTENCY. Going and sowing week in and week out. Those who are the most consistent in going out to sow seem to bear the most fruit. Over the years I've read several books that have challenged and helped me in the area of evangelism. *The General Next To God, The Cross And The Switchblade* and *Just Off Chicken Street*, just to name a few. The people of these books had one thing in common. They had a consistent determination to reach their world for Jesus. They maintained a high visibility into the area they were reaching into on a constant basis. They also invested much time and effort sometimes for weeks, months or years with little or no visible fruit. They were sowers of the highest order. Yet, in time the harvest came, souls were saved, people were delivered from drugs and alcohol, and churches were built. They were determined and did not give up.

Also, of the growing churches I have heard and read about today who are effective in reaching the lost, again *consistency* seems to be one of the keys. They have made a quality decision to pay the price to be there in all seasons.

A missionary friend of mine, while on furlough, began to help establish a street outreach in Toledo, Ohio. They began by praying about the area and felt they were to go to a block in the downtown district. Prostitutes and night people were the order of the day. They set up a small caravan in a parking lot as a base and brought the contacts to it for talks and coffee. They went every Friday night for several months. Initially, not much headway was made, but seeds were sown. Now, after much sowing, the harvest is being reaped! People are coming to know Jesus, are being added to the church and other churches are now interested and taking part. Again, one of the keys for their success is CONSISTENCY.

As a word of caution, it is important to know that sowing seeds as a corporate body should never be seen to be the end of our personal sowing. Sometimes we think that if we have helped at a fellowship function or an open-air then we've done our bit of sowing for the month. This is the one danger that can come to a body of believers as they reach out together. We should always view this type of sowing as *stepping stones* to help us to become greater seed sowers.

For example, helping in an open-air outreach should help us to develop confidence, boldness, and security in the Lord as we sow seeds together. This in turn should help us to sow as we go about our personal daily lives. As the opportunity arises to share our faith, we can share with greater confidence because we have already had the experience of sowing within the security of a larger group.

Does this type of corporate sowing work for you there in Scotland? I mean aren't you just a small church not a mega one? Isn't success measured in numbers? Numbers are important, I'll admit. However, as the saying goes, Rome was not built in a day. We have had to begin where we are. Just as you will have to begin where you are. *Smallness should never become an excuse for not going and sowing.* Month by month we have been sowing in faith, and we have reaped. People have come to know Jesus, the gospel has been proclaimed, the church has been established, our visibility as a church has been raised in our community, and again, many, many seeds have been sown—corporate seeds that may one day bear fruit.

7

Seeds Individually

We all have seeds that we can sow as individuals into the lives of our friends, families, workmates and the strangers we meet. We might not be aware that we have them, but we do. I would like to look at three of the most powerful seeds that you personally can sow.

The word of our testimony

Our testimony is probably one of the most powerful tools that we can ever use in sowing the gospel. It is the one thing about us that people cannot refute. Many have tried to tell me that what happened to me was no more than my mind, some figment of my imagination. My testimony declares there to be more to it than this, as does my changed life; and no one can change this reality.

Many of the sermons in the book of Acts are testimony—men simply declaring what had happened to them. Peter on the day of Pentecost declared, *'This* (you see and hear) *is what was spoken by the prophet Joel'* (a demonstration of what God said would happen) (Acts 2:16, NIV).

The early disciples also declared to the opposing religious leaders of the day, '... *We cannot help speaking about what we have **seen** and **heard'** (Acts 4:20, NIV).

What they saw and heard they spoke about / testified to. This is what they experienced when they were with Jesus.

45

(See 1 John 1:1–3.) The leaders of the day did note that they were unlearned men and that they had been with Him. Their words and lives again testified to this fact.

When Paul was confronted and had to give a defence for the hope he had within him, he simply declared what had happened to him (his testimony, see Acts 22 and Acts 26). His testimony had such power that King Agrippa exclaimed,

> *Do you think that in such a short time you can persuade me to be a Christian?* (Acts 26:28, NIV)

Also, the Gospels are really just testimonies of Matthew, Mark, Luke and John.

In John's gospel we can see the impact of a personal testimony on an entire town. A woman gave a simple declaration about Jesus and what had happened when He had spoken to her.

In John, Chapter 4, Jesus confronted the woman at the well. As He spoke to her, He was bringing greater and greater revelation of who He really was. At one point Jesus asked the lady to go call her husband. She replied that she had no husband. Jesus then spoke a word of knowledge that she had lived with at least five men and the man she now lived with was not her husband. She then perceived that He was more than a man—that He was a prophet. She was later told that He was the Christ. She was so moved by this encounter that she left her water pot and went back to the town where she had come from. At this point she gave her testimony to the people.

> *Come see a man who told me everything I ever did. Could this be the Christ?* (John 4:29, NIV)

Now Jesus had not told her *'everything'* she had ever done, but just enough to let her know that He knew. The result of her short testimony was that *'Many of the*

Samaritans from that town believed in Him...' and they asked Jesus to stay with them for two days. '*...and because of His words many more became believers. They said to the woman, 'We no longer believe just because of what you said; now we have heard for ourselves, and we know that this man really is the Saviour of the world'* (John 4:39–42, NIV).

Her simple testimony had the power to draw men to Jesus. Then they were able to hear for themselves, and by hearing they believed. The word of our testimony has this kind of power, the 'If it happened to you, maybe it could happen to me' kind of power, the 'If Jesus is the answer for you, perhaps He is the answer for me' kind of power.

I don't believe we really know just what powerful seeds our individual testimonies can be. Many have said, 'I just don't have a great testimony like Joe Smoe. I mean, I haven't killed anyone, I wasn't involved with drugs or wild sex. I wasn't a Hell's Angel. I was just a normal person.' Well, there are a whole lot of normal people out there who need to hear that normal people can come to know Jesus. Your testimony is powerful! Don't listen to the lies that tell you that your testimony is not important. Speak up, sow the seed and watch what happens! You'll be amazed!

Many, also, miss the fact that our testimonies are always changing. Daily, Jesus meets our needs. He heals our bodies, provides for us, protects us, and speaks to us. If there is no update in what God is both saying and doing for us as individuals and as a church, there is something wrong somewhere. As He lives with us and in us, so should our lives be changing, our prayers should be answered, we should be growing from faith to faith, and our testimonies should reflect this reality now.

When speaking to people outside the Kingdom of God, I tell them that for 22 years I refused to acknowledge that there was a personal God with a personal plan for my life. Therefore, I tried (in vain I might add) to find evidence to deny His existence in order to absolve any of my account-ability to Him. Now, however, for these past 16 years I have been gaining living evidence that He does exist and is indeed interested in my life. I testify to this by telling people just what God has done for me and my family. The provisions I've received at just the right times, the healings I've seen, the awareness of sin forgiven and the words I've heard Him speak. Because He is alive and I am learning to walk with Him, I am gaining fresh testimony and insight almost daily. These up to date testimonies declare to the world that my God is much more than an idea or an impersonal force. They declare His interest, care and concern. His reality! All of us, if we know Him, can openly testify to these things.

Jesus is interested in us all from the youngest child to the oldest man or woman. We were all sinners needing a Lord and Saviour. Jesus is the answer for our lives and our testi-monies declare this to be true. Jesus has saved us. He has made us new creations. There is more to life now. We do have a purpose and a destiny. We do know why we are here, where we came from, and where we are going. We have peace because we are at peace with our Creator. We are secure in an insecure world because He holds all things together by His power. We are known by Him and we are coming to know Him more day by day. Our lives and lips testify and point to this truth powerfully.

The word of our testimony has life within it. Revelation 12:11 declares,

> *They overcame him* [the devil] *by the blood of the Lamb and **by the word of their testimony**; they did not love their lives so much as to shrink from death.* (NIV)

The enemy would like us to keep quiet about the good-ness of our God. Yet, we can rise up and speak forth the word of our testimony to sow seeds into the lives of men and women. This defeats the enemy by bringing men progressively from darkness into light. We, also, overcome him by reminding ourselves and declaring to others what God has done and is doing for us. We gain encouragement when we testify, and God calls it faith. This is called *'The word of our testimony.'* This is what we speak, and as we speak, we overcome.

Larry Tomczak, who is a well known author, church planter and evangelist in the USA, has encouraged his hearers and readers for years to write their own personal tract to give to people they meet. Several years ago I did this and have given it to hundreds of people I have come in contact with, from supermarket check-out ladies, waiters and waitresses, to teenagers I've met in the street. I have never had a refusal when I tell them, 'Here's the story of my life.' Most are amazed that this is the same person talking to them. Many times they want to talk more. Yet, even if they don't I know a seed has been sown. Like I said, 'Our testimonies are powerful seeds!' You have one, why not begin to use it!

Signs and wonders

Jesus throughout His ministry allowed signs and wonders to testify about Him. They were stepping stones of faith for both His disciples and unbelievers alike. The Gospel of John points out some of these signs and wonders which declare that Jesus is the Christ.

> *Jesus did many other miraculous signs in the presence of His disciples, which are not recorded in this book. But these* [signs and wonders] *are written* [Why?] *that you may believe that Jesus is the Christ, the Son of God and that believing you may have life in His name.*
>
> (John 20:30–31)

49

I will run briefly through the book of John giving an overview of the signs and wonders Jesus did and the results.

John 1:43–50...Jesus and Nathanael.
  Sign: Word of Knowledge, 'I saw you...'
  Result: 'You are the Son of God.'

John 2:1–11...Wedding at Cana.
  Sign: Miracle, 'Water to wine.'
  Result: 'His disciples put their faith in Him.'

John 4:4–42...Jesus and a woman at a well.
  Sign: Word of Knowledge, 'The fact is you have had five husbands the man you now have is not your husband.'
  Result: 'Women and men of the town believe in Jesus.'

John 9:1–41...Jesus and the blind man.
  Sign: Healing, 'Blind man receives His sight.'
  Result: 'Man believes, religious leaders confronted.'

John 11:15–45...Jesus and Lazarus.
  Sign: Miracle, 'Lazarus is raised from the dead after four days.'
  Result: 'Many who had visited Mary put their faith in Him.'

All of these were stepping-stones to faith for many people. Whenever there was a sign or wonder, the goal was that people might come to believe in Him. They were indeed stepping-stones to faith for many, yet stumbling-blocks for some.

Jesus, when challenged by the unbelieving Jews, simply replied by pointing to the signs and wonders He was doing.

> *The miracles I do in my Father's name speak for me...Do not believe me* [my words] *unless I do what my Father does* [works]. *But if I do it, even though you do not believe me* [my words], **believe the miracles** [works], *that you may* **know** *and* **understand** *that the*

Father is in me, and I in the Father.

(John 10:25,37–38, NIV)

In other words Jesus was saying,

> *If you don't believe my words, believe the signs and wonders. They declare to you who I am.* (John 5:36)

This was to be *one* of the reasons for them to believe, the signs and wonders. Yet, they were so hardened in their hearts that they were blinded to the reality of the life and power of God the signs and wonders revealed.

Jesus also encouraged His disciples to believe that He was the Christ through this ministry of signs and wonders. Philip said,

> *Lord, show us the Father and that will be enough for us.*

Jesus answered:

> *Don't you know me, Philip, even after I have been among you for such a long time? Any one who has seen me has seen the Father. How can you say, 'Show us the Father?' Don't you believe that I am in the Father, and that the Father is in Me? The words I say to you are not just my own. Rather, it is the Father, living in me, who is doing His work. Believe me when I say that I am in the Father and the Father is in Me; or **at least believe on the evidence of the miracles themselves*** (John 14:8–11).

Here the disciples are. Jesus has been with them for three years and He is about to go to the Father in a few days. He is giving them last minute instructions, speaking to them about His death and another Comforter who will be both in and with them. They still haven't understood who He is. (I'm amazed that Jesus didn't hit His forehead in exasperation.

51

Maybe He did!?) To highlight who he was, He simply pointed back to the signs and wonders that He had done in their midst. He encouraged them to remember the lame that walked, the blind that began to see, the lepers that were cleansed, the demons that were cast out, the feeding of the multitudes, and the dead that were raised.

Many of the disciples probably had their own personal miracle that reinforced their belief that He was the Christ. For Peter, it may have been the great catch of fish or the time he walked on the water with Him. The other disciples were probably running their own video tapes in their minds of other signs and wonders that impressed them. This may have caused faith to rise in their hearts, confirming again their belief that Jesus was indeed the Christ.

He also said,

> *I tell you the truth, anyone who has faith in me **will do** what I have been doing. He will do **even greater things** than these, because I am going to the Father.*
>
> (John 14:12, NIV)

The book of Acts proves that His disciples and others did the things Jesus did in the area of signs and wonders. People were healed, others were raised from the dead, demons were cast out and even Peter's shadow falling upon people healed the sick (a greater thing?).

Also, Jesus, by the power of His Holy Spirit, is continuing to do mighty signs and wonders in our day. Many books have been written documenting many wonderful healings and other signs over the past and recent years showing that God's power is still at work in the earth.

Driving through a wealthy city in south Florida one spring, I observed much materialism, drunkenness, lust and sin. It seemed to me that everyone was looking out for number one and living for the day. 'Eat drink and be merry for tomorrow you will die' seemed to be the spirit of the area. I remember asking my wife and Jesus, 'How can anyone blast through all this stuff to cause people to be awakened to their sin and their need for Jesus?' Two thoughts came into my mind, one was the judgement of God, and the second was God's power being released through signs and wonders. I believe it will probably take both, along with much grace and mercy.

Signs and wonders are needed like never before to break into the lives of lost men and women. They need to understand that 'God' is not merely a religious idea, nor a cosmic impersonal force but He is living, and He will reward everyone according to their deeds. He also is loving and kind and desires all people to come to know Him in a personal way through Jesus Christ. They need to see by demonstration that He is active and is able and willing to heal their bodies and to deliver them from addictive habits, from depression and from other afflicting ailments that bind them. They need to know that He is also able to save forever all who come to Him.

As a side note, the world also needs to see the church being the church, not just a building or a meeting to attend, but to see the church as a people who are enthused and infused with the life of Jesus. A people who are indeed 'the called out ones' who are different then the normal in life and action—a people who are 'ruined for the ordinary', who have tasted the life to come, who have a calling to fulfil, and a sense of purpose and a destiny. I believe that the world is waiting for such a people to appear, as is the Father. It is heartening to know that all over the world the restoration of the church is in process. People are catching the vision of just what the church is really supposed to be and are becoming more and more committed to this dynamic life-changing vision.

Over the past few years, we as a church, have seen many people moved to faith in Jesus through signs and wonders, while others have only acknowledged that God was among us.

Several years ago, we felt we were to go to the surrounding towns of our area and do an outreach evening. In one town, we went to every door with invitations and spent time on the streets speaking to people and inviting them to come along. During preparation for the evening I was waiting on the Lord and asked Him what He wanted to do that evening. I had an impression that there would be a lady there who had a pain in her right shoulder and that it was arthritic. I thought that it might be the Lord or my lunch. I chose to believe that it was the Lord, being the great man of paste and flour that I am. That evening, to say the least, was a bit of a disappointment. I think that about 10 people came who were not from our church. I preached a short message and then began to 'move' in the gifts. I now was going to see if it was the Lord or lunch. Hey, I mean, I was a real man of faith. I asked, with much unbelief, 'Is there anyone here with a sore shoulder?' To my surprise a lady raised her hand. I then asked, with a little more faith, 'Is it your right shoulder?' She said it was. I then knew that I really did hear from the Lord, so now boldly asked and with authority, 'Is it arthritic?' She replied that it was. I said, 'Come on down!' I don't know who was more excited, she or I. I didn't even get to pray for her. Others who were helping in the outreach did. She not only got healed instantly, but she met Jesus that night. The evening very quickly changed from a disappointment to an encouraging stepping stone in our lives. Now, her daughter and son are believers and I have grown in faith.

One evening a girl came for prayer. She had hurt her foot in gymnastics and had a competition coming up and wanted to be healed. She was not a believer but had heard that we regularly pray for the sick. She received prayer and Jesus healed her. She later won her gymnastics trial. A seed was sown. Later, her mum also came for prayer. She had had kidney problems and also asked to be healed. She received prayer and instantly the pain which had been with her for some time left. Two days later the pain came back. She simply said, 'No, I've been healed!' the pain immediately left and to my knowledge has not returned. Later, we were called to come and pray for a lady she worked for. During the many visits I was able to tell her the real reason Jesus had healed her, that He was interested in her life and wanted her whole in spirit, soul and body. Even though she has not made Jesus had Lord yet, a seed has been sown! She can now never deny that God exists or that He is not interested in her life and family. (Note too, how their testimonies were being sown from family members to friends even though they were unsaved.)

It may amaze many that some of the people who are healed physically do not always come to Jesus to be saved. (One young man I know was healed of colour blindness, a dislocated shoulder, and a cracked knee cap, yet He still chose to stop following Jesus.) I too, often pondered this until I read where Jesus said to the seventy who were sent out,

> *Heal the sick who are there and tell them, 'The kingdom of God is **near** you'.* (Luke 10:9, NIV, emphasis mine)

He didn't say that those who were healed were in the Kingdom automatically but that the Kingdom of God had come near to them. They still had to make a choice to allow Jesus to be Lord of their lives. This truth remains the same today. Nevertheless, deep seeds are planted when people are confronted with the power of God. They are also moved along the scale into saving faith more quickly.

We always need to look for the opportunity to pray for the lost. It might be for something as small as a headache or as large as cancer. Whatever the need may be, we simply need to be obedient to the Holy Spirit's prompting. As we step out in faith, we then give God opportunity to move through us. When He moves through us, people are touched and drawn to Jesus. *Signs and wonders are powerful seeds indeed!*

The Gospel Seed

If we share our testimonies, pray for the sick, friendship evangelise and sow many different seeds into the lives of the lost there is still one missing seed, the most powerful, the 'Gospel Seed'.

It is by the preaching of the cross that people come to saving faith. *It has always been God's way and it will always be!*

All of the other methods and means will not bring people to saving faith *until* they hear the good news of Jesus Christ. This we need to understand!

Many have had 'friendship evangelism' going on for years and maybe wondered why so few have become believers. If they would check, it just might be they have neglected to share the good news of the cross with the hearers on a consistent basis. The people they are attempting to reach will be drawn and their hearts made receptive through their friendship, but they will not be able to be born again and enter into the Kingdom of God unless they hear and understand the good news. *'How, then, can they call on the one they have not believed in?* **They can't!** *And how can they believe in the one of whom they have not heard?* **They can't!** *And how can they hear without some preaching to them?* **They can't!** *And how can they preach unless they are sent?* **We are sent!'** (Romans 10:14–15, NIV)

Paul declared,

> *I am not ashamed of the gospel, for it is the power of God for the salvation of everyone who believes: first for the Jew, then for the Gentile.* (Romans 1:16, NIV)

The gospel has power in itself. When the cross is proclaimed and understood, salvation is made available to the hearer. Paul also said,

> *The message of the cross is foolishness to those who are perishing, but to us who are being saved it is the power of God.... God was well-pleased through the foolishness of what was preached to save those who believe.... We preach Christ crucified.... Christ the power of God and the wisdom of God.* (1 Corinthians 1:18–25, NIV)

The reason the great evangelists of the past and of our day have such success is because they present the cross simply, clearly, and powerfully. Billy Graham is one of these evangelists who has remained faithful to the preaching of the cross. The fruit of this message is there for all to see.

The message of the early church was also clear and to the point: Jesus and Him crucified for your sin. He bore your judgement. He paid the penalty due to you. He demonstrated the love and justice of God. He died. He was buried. He rose again. He entered into heaven itself to appear before God on your behalf, carrying His own Blood to be given as a perfect sacrifice for your sins. If you trust in, rely on and cling to Him as Lord and Saviour you will be saved. This was their distinct word to the hearers.

They proclaimed, with Paul,

> *The word is near you; it is in your mouth, and in your heart, 'that is the word of faith' we are proclaiming: That if you confess with your mouth, 'Jesus is Lord,' and believe in your heart that God raised Him from the dead, you will be saved.* (Romans 10:9–10, NIV)

Remember,

> *Faith comes from hearing the message, and the message*

is heard through the word of Christ.

(Romans 10:17, NIV)

They can hear the good news through a preacher at a meeting, through someone in the street, through a friend or through a tract. But, until people hear the gospel message they *cannot be saved*. This is why the message of the cross is the most powerful seed! We need to proclaim it boldly and without shame!

Seeds

These are just a few of the seeds we can sow into the lives of people we are in contact with daily. If we are creative and are endeavouring to sow consistently, evangelism can become exciting to us as we begin to see our part in God's wonderful plan for man. We will be sowing in faith, looking for the harvest and rejoicing when the harvest does come.

8

Today!

In our culture it is the thought of many that, 'Jesus will save me if He wants to.' This thought is related to the extreme teaching of the sovereignty of God. This kind of thinking was/is the thinking that hindered evangelism and world missions yesterday and hinders evangelism and world missions today. It is the thinking that says, 'If God wants to save the world He is quite able to do it without your help.' This thinking flows over into the thought life of some of the people we are trying to reach. However, the Word of God says:

> *In the time of favour I heard you, and in the day of salvation I helped you. Now is the time of God's favour, Now is the day of salvation.* (2 Corinthians 6:2, NIV)

Everyday is the day of salvation for those who choose to allow Jesus to become Lord of their lives. *Everyday* is the day that Jesus wants to come into the lives of those who ask Him, bringing with Him salvation, wholeness, health and eternal life. Many may need to be challenged that *this* day is *the* day for them. That *this time* is *the time* for them to call upon the name of the Lord.

Those who are reapers usually sense when to press toward a decision on behalf of the Lord. They realise that the seed has been sown, watered and is now ready for harvest. This may come just after an evangelistic message has been clearly preached, or maybe the person has been witnessed to over a period of time. Nevertheless, they clearly bring the challenge of salvation being *today*, *now*, and readily available at *this present time* to the individual. All that is now needed is a response in faith from the hearer. Their response is all important. It is based on what they have heard and understood (see Mark 4). Remember,

> *Faith comes from hearing the message, and the message is heard through the word of Christ.*
>
> (Romans 10:17, NIV)

This response is a response of heart belief and vocal confession. When this combination is meant, by faith, and vocalised through prayer, people become saved or born again. When this decision comes and is acted upon in a point in time, for them, it is *the time* and it is *the day* of salvation. The word of faith says... *'The word is near you; it is in your mouth and in your heart,'* that is, the word of faith we are proclaiming:*That if you confess with your mouth, 'Jesus is Lord,' and believe in your heart that God raised him from the dead, you will be saved. For it is with your heart that you believe and are justified, and it is with your mouth that you confess and are saved...*

> *Everyone who calls on the name of the Lord will be saved.* (Romans 10:8–10,13, NIV)

We need to always be ready to say, *'Today* is *the day* for you!'

A young man had been attending our meetings for several weeks. His parents were both Christians as were many of his friends. Deep seeds had been sown and watered. I began to wonder, 'When is this guy going to meet Jesus and be born again?' After a Sunday gathering, I approached him and asked, 'When are you going to give your life to Jesus?' He replied, 'Whenever He wants me to be saved I'll be saved.' It then dawned upon me that he was waiting for a voice from heaven, or a blinding light to knock him down, or something to cause him to come to saving faith. He had somehow picked up this concept that God, being totally sovereign, would save him if and when He wanted to. I then began to share with him concerning our choice and our part we have to play in God's plan of Salvation. I also briefly explained the free will of man, and that God was a whosoever God. I then showed him that *now* could be *the time* and *the day* for him. Graciously, he saw. Lights went on! Revelation came, and he understood that Jesus had died for his sins and that he could be saved right then, at that moment. I asked if he wanted to pray, and he did. Jesus fulfilled His Word! He came to him, and the young man was wonderfully born again to a living hope. He entered into the life long process of salvation. For him, that day was *the time* and *the day* of salvation. He was overjoyed, as were his parents, and I'm sure many angels in heaven!

Remember, many people we talk to in the Scottish/European culture have this mindset. They need to know that *today* can be *the day* for them. In all of our sowing, we need to continually bring to people, this wonderful concept of TODAY!

9

Said And Done

As the saying goes, 'When all is said and done there is usually more said than done.' The 90's are upon us, and many have declared this to be the 'Decade of Evangelism'; and it very well may be. There will probably be more conferences telling us how to do evangelism than ever before. Yet, until we begin to do evangelism, it remains theory and a good and noble thought. James exhorts us,

> *Do not merely listen to the word, and so deceive yourselves. Do what it says.* (James 1:22, NIV)

This is the real way we learn to reach others for Jesus, by doing it. We do need teaching and training, yet, going forth untrained will train us and we will learn as the disciples learned, through their mistakes, failures and successes. Every step we take to reach out will bring to us greater wisdom, understanding and ability to share our faith with others.

When do you need to begin? Right now! As you take faltering steps, you will gain courage and will see that evangelism isn't as hard as the devil tells you. There really are people out there who are wanting to know about Jesus, and you do have good news to share. Now is the time to begin. Don't wait! Make plans to talk to your neighbour, to join a street team, to go to your local youth club with the express purpose of sharing Jesus or to share your faith with your workmates. Making your mind up to go is more than half of the battle; opening your mouth is the second half. Every time I go out to share my faith, I find myself nervous, unsure and at times fearful. Most of the time I don't feel like going. However, as I chose to go and to take the first step by opening my mouth, the anxiety just melts away. As I go forth, there are times when I have great talks, and then there are other times when I open my mouth that I sound like I'm saying, 'gubber gobbly gook mutter mutter.' Nevertheless, I always learn something from the experience which equips me for the next opportunity.

Every believer needs to begin *now. Now* is the time to go, to begin to learn to reach others effectively for Jesus.

Helpful hints

Here are some helpful hints to help you to get going.

Smile! What you have is the good news! You are in the Kingdom of God where there is *'righteousness, peace and joy in the Holy Ghost'* (Romans 14:17, NIV). You have been set free and can share this freedom *joyfully*!

Recently a group from the church went swimming and the ticket lady was 'peopled out'. Suddenly, 63 Christians arrived. They were smiling, friendly and actually talked with her. She was uplifted and commented the next day to the other workers how nice it was to actually be smiled at and treated well.

Listen! As you begin your conversation, take an interest in them. Show this interest by looking them in the face and by listening, not thinking about what you will share next. Take a mental note of their name and what they enjoy doing. Many doors are opened as you simply talk to them about their favourite subject, them. Ask them about themselves, what they like to do, their families, or their hobbies. You then gain the right to speak to them.

If I go and get a hair cut I almost always come home bald. It seems that once I begin talking about their profession and family, they almost always begin to ask me questions. I use this time for an opportunity to share my faith. As you learn the art of listening, many doors will also open for you to share your faith.

Admit! Many times I get put in a situation where I don't know the answer for tough questions. When this happens I simply admit that I don't know the answer. Admitting that you don't know the answer at the present time, really does gain favour with most people. They expect Christians to be honest and are impressed when they are, and are not given the run around. You can always make an appointment with them later to share your findings after you have researched their question.

Stick to Jesus! Rabbit trails are interesting and can be fun or they can be wearing. Remember to always come back to Jesus, who He is and what He has done. Jesus is always the central issue and what they think of Him and what they will do with Him. Tell them about Him, how He saved you, how He treated people during His earthly ministry, how and why He died, and how He is coming back as King of Kings and Lord of Lords to rule and reign in the earth. They most probably have not heard much of this before. Remember,

> *Salvation is found in no one else, for there is no other name under heaven given to men by which we must be saved.* (Acts 4:12, NIV)

It is this Jesus we want them to meet.

Stay informed! What in the world is happening? Do you know? Keep up to date on current affairs of your town, country and the world. What does the Bible say about the signs of the times? If you are ministering to certain people groups, do research into that group. For example, if you are attempting to reach teens, read teen magazines, check out the words to the latest songs and ask questions concerning the latest styles and fads. What is Acid House? What is a NED or a Causal? Jason who? What New Kids Are On whose Block anyway? Being informed can open many doors to share your faith.

Recently, my next door neighbour was working on his motorcycle. I began to talk to him about motorcycles. I don't know much about them but I do know what a Harley is and have ridden one before. Believe it or not, it opened doors for me to speak to him for some time and helped to build a bridge for future conversations.

Be determined! This is a key to keep you going on a consistent basis. Plan to go, and be determined that nothing will get in the way of your plans. Do what you have determined to do. Go where you have determined to go. Swear to your own hurt. If you have said you will go, Go! It is amazing how many things do come up after I've planned to go talk to a neighbour, to go to an open-air meeting or to go to the Inverness Youth For Christ coffee bar. It is determination that gets me there.

Pray! As we pray we will begin to sense God's heart and priority for the world. Prayer is the one way to draw God toward men and men toward God. Intercede for those you are trying to reach. Ask the Holy Spirit to send you to harvest people and pray for divine appointments, then put feet to your prayers, go, and watch God use you.

Develop sensitivity! Learn to listen to the Holy Spirit. He does want to speak to you and to the person you are talking to. Ask Him silent questions as you are listening or talking to the person. 'What is the greatest need of this person at this time? Is there anything you want me to know? What do you want me to say? Should I offer to pray for them Lord? Do you want them healed? Do you have any words of knowledge or other gifts of the Spirit for this person?'

Mike, the leader of the openair team in Dunfermline, was travelling on a train in London recently. Among the crowd there was a lady with a baby. He felt drawn to her and began to quietly pray, 'Lord, what do you want me to do?' 'Pray for the baby!' was the reply. Here he was on a train overflowing with people, and he was supposed to pray? What did he do? He simply obeyed. He began a conversation with the lady and found out that she had brought the baby from Ireland to London for health reasons. Mike took a risk and asked if he could pray for the baby. The woman was overjoyed! She related to him that she was recently thinking how she really would have liked her priest to be there to pray for her and the child. Mike then asked for permission to place his hand on the baby and prayed. He doesn't know if the baby was healed or not but had a great talk with the mother. He also had a real sense of fulfilment simply because he was sensitive and obeyed the prompting of the Holy Spirit.

Doers

The challenge to the church in these days is to be those who do evangelism and not those who just talk about evangelism. This decade can be an exciting one for us as we go with the good news. Our lives and the lives around us can be changed as we become 'doers'. Begin now! Take a step of faith! Open your mouth and begin to spread the gospel seed and become a joyful sower!

When all is said and done, I pray that more is done than said.

'Father. Send us to harvest people. Your word says, 'No one can come to Jesus unless the Father draws them.' So send us to the people you are drawing. Allow us to co-work with you in sowing your seeds into the hearts of men and women. Father, bring the increase.'

Amen!

10

Sample Testimony Tract

Hi! My name is Steve and I come from the USA. I have been in Scotland now for about 13 years working with young people and sharing my life I have found in Jesus.

This exciting walk I now have with the living God through Jesus all started about 18 years ago.

The late 1960's and the early 70's were turbulent years for the USA and myself. I was involved in the drug culture of that era and all that it contained. Rebellion against authority, lust and the party life. My life began to fall into trouble not long after my drug involvement. My family life was a mess and so I tried to stay in with the in crowd and be accepted. It was at this time I began to see the shallowness of the drug scene but somehow did not have the power nor the desire to stop. Besides it did have a degree of acceptance, fun and excitement. Suddenly my life really did fall apart...

I received in the post my draft notice that I was to report for Army service. I knew that this meant Vietnam and fighting in the war. Some of my friends wanted me to go to Canada and hide until the war was over. I chose, however, to join the US Navy. I did and found that I had more unrest inside. I continued in late night parties, drink and drug abuse. It was after 2 years in the Navy stationed in Florida that my life really began to deteriorate. I found it harder and harder to maintain rational thinking and my physical body also began to suffer.

Then I met Tim who was a real Christian. He began to tell

me about Jesus and what He could do for me. I used to listen to him, ask questions and tell him my ideas about God. As a result my thinking began to change. I realised tht if God was indeed God and Jesus was who he said He was, then, if I became a believer, I would have to be a real one and not play church or games with God. I saw the cost. At this time, however, I was not ready to give up my lifestyle and continued on in drinking, parties and drugs.

During the next few months it was as if I was on a slide to torment. My parents were divorced, which I thought was partly my fault; other relationships that I was trying to build fell apart and I was once again finding it hard to cope with guilt and my problems.

I left Florida to try and get away from it all and went to my home in Kentucky. It was while there that my life almost came to an end. At a party someone offered me some hard drugs which I willingly took. It was a bad batch and I ended up overdosed (not for the first time), facing death and looking eternity in the face. I was in bad shape!

Then, I remembered some of what Tim had told me concerning Jesus and God the Father. I realised that I needed Him to save my life and give me a new beginning. I understood the cost, that it was all for Him or nothing. I then simply cried from the depths of my heart, 'God help me!' To my amazement His power and presence came to me that night and I knew that everything would be alright. Later the same week a man I met told me more about Jesus and how HE could save me. It was at this time that I asked Jesus to come into my life and to be the boss. He did and my life has never been the same. He has given me fulfilment in every area of my life. I have come to realise that God is indeed a good God who desires the highest good of every living thing. The mess we find our lives in is not the result of a mean God but the direct result of our own selfishness and sin. However, Jesus is in the restoration business and offers new life to those who will pay the price to give their lives to Him.

We live in exciting times and God is on the Move. Jesus' return is near. I would encourage you to think more about this Jesus you have been reading about and even to give your life to Him. He offers life to the fullest to you!